Will our childr

GW01466403

OH LORD - .... .
FOR THE TIME
TO RAISE THE
ISSUE OF
FAMILY PRAYER...

WiLL OUR CHiLDREN HAVE FAMiLY PRAYER?

Clare Maloney

VERITAS

First published 1999 by
Veritas Publications
7/8 Lower Abbey Street
Dublin 1

Copyright © Clare Maloney

ISBN 1 85390 404 X

Design: Bill Bolger
Cover photographs: Clare Maloney
Cartoons: John Byrne
Printed in Ireland by Betaprint Ltd, Dublin

CONTENTS

Introduction

My thoughts on family prayer are the thoughts of a parent with four children; one in primary school, two in secondary school and one in third level. I represent that parental age group who may now be in their early forties; those who were the children of the sixties, teenagers of the seventies and young parents of the eighties. I myself was married in June 1979, the year in which the country turned out en masse for the papal visit. Being from the North of Ireland, and living as I then did, near Drogheda, our house was full beyond capacity with relatives and friends, old and young, who had journeyed south for the occasion. Much has happened in the twenty years since then and one wonders if that papal visit might not, in retrospect, have been a 'grand finale', marking the end of an era. If it did, then it is, roughly speaking, my age group of parent who bridges the gap between that era and the next. We are old enough to have experienced the television being switched off as everyone knelt down for the rosary. We are young enough to be part of the decline in regular attendance at mass. By and large it is we who are the parents of the children now exiting the church or, if I might put it differently, 'making a new Church Exodus'.

This booklet is aimed at parents who suspect that prayer in the life of a family would be a good thing, but find it difficult to take the matter any further. It is aimed at parents who are so busy just keeping the family show-on-the-road, that they haven't the energy to stop and think about prayer – though they would probably agree that it would be a good thing to do. To parents such as these, I hope this booklet may offer practical help and motivation to start, or re-start, family prayer.

One of the difficulties with family prayer is that it is not individual prayer. It must offer something – a language, a structure, a ritual – which can be personal and which speaks to and for each individual family member, but can also be more than personal. Family prayer is more complex than 'my personal relationship with God'; it is about the jumble – or 'jungle' - of internal relationships in a family and the relationship of all of that to God and to the world. To find prayerful expression of this is not easy but the rosary did offer a kind of model. It was an example of a prayer with a common language with which everyone felt at home –the Hail Mary. It had a substantial structure – the five decades and their 'trimmings'. It also had ritual – the kneeling down and the processing of the beads through the fingers. The extinction of such a 'solid' family prayer form has left us with a blank; with literally nothing to say; speechless. When we go to Mass, which is probably for most people the main act of prayer in their lives, we encounter another example of a prayer ritual which still offers these things. But by and large we find that we must leave our homes in order to do this. In other words, our most visible form of prayer happens *outside* of our own kitchens and living rooms. We arrive in a building where everything in relation to prayer is foreknown, i.e. the what, when, why and where of praying is all taken care of. We have learned responses, so we know what words to say and when to say them. We know when to sit or stand or kneel and we do these things in the confines of a building in which everyone else is doing the same thing at the same time. The various symbols – candle, crucifix, vestments, music, etc. are familiar and comfortable, 'furnishing' the whole experience in a non-domestic fashion. And to the extent that we encounter silence within these liturgical occasions, it is a silence we can be comfortable with.

At home, on the other hand, we tend to find ourselves 'vacant' in relation to prayer. When should we do it? Where should we do it? What should we say? Who should take the lead? How long should it last? What should it be about? What if we get it wrong? What if the kids laugh? What if one or other partner is dubious or reticent, or simply not interested? What if they refuse to take part? What if it is such an embarrassing, cringing, 'The Waltons' type experience that no one will risk doing it again? And perhaps the most daunting question of all, 'What if there's dead silence?' These are very real questions for today's parents, old and young.

This booklet will try to encourage and support parents by offering something of substance, form and structure, with which families may begin to fill the vacuum left by the rosary; a kind of 'homemade prayer recipe'. I have chosen the word recipe not just for its domestic connotations, but more importantly because, in its oldest form, the word was associated with the formula for a medical prescription, or the remedy prepared in accordance with this. I have also chosen it because recipes are things which require making if they are to become real – not just pictures in a book. (Prayer, I believe, is a 'making' as much as a saying). Once made, recipes become food, which may feed a hungry family, in this instance food for families who have a hunger that prayer and only prayer may satisfy. This book, like all recipe books, requires that you check ingredients, methods, cooking times, and the practicality and suitability in terms of the tastes of your particular family. The recipes are intended to be down-to-earth. But, just as no one ever makes a recipe exactly as it is in the book, these recipes will prove most beneficial if they are adapted to the needs of the individual family, of which you the reader have the fullest knowledge. They are therefore only half the story: you the reader, are the other half. But before getting into the detail of the recipes, the following general hints may be worth considering:

HINTS

Be Patient

Most of us carry a lot of unfortunate baggage when it comes to prayer. We may have a lot more negative than positive experiences to build on when it comes to praying, so if mistakes are made – and they will be – we need to be patient with ourselves.

Patience needs to be extended to others as well. It is unlikely that both people in a partnership, or all those in a family, will be on equal terms when it comes to prayer. It is 'unprayerful' to force or coerce people to participate if they are not yet ready to do so. A much better experience for them would be to realise that they can take responsibility for when they do or don't pray. Thus a person may eventually arrive at a point where – although he or she may not feel like praying – with due negotiation, they are prepared to override their feelings for the sake of others who would appreciate their participation.

Don't Underestimate Yourself

Given the strangeness of the task of conducting (in the sense of being a conductor, as in electricity) family prayer, it would be understandable to think that there are others who would do this much better than oneself. This may or may not be true, but the chances are that the desire to find an expert is a desire to escape to a situation where someone else will tell you what to do, or what to say. I would like to point out that I am no expert on the matter of family prayer, but an interested contributor to what might be a stage in its development at this critical point in history. Indeed, I have made a deliberate choice not to consult the experts – the writings of saints, mystics, theologians, etc. – in order not to undermine the embryonic sense of family authority for family prayer.

Will Our Children Have Family Prayer?   5

Make the most of 'Ingredients you already have in the Cupboard'
One of the things I have always admired about my mother is her capacity to work the on-going miracle of the loaves and fishes. Opening the cupboard and protesting, 'There's not a bite in the house!' she nevertheless consistently managed to make dinner or tea for a hungry family, or a tasty snack for an unexpected visitor. Given the history of the practice of prayer in our lives, it is not surprising that, in the absence of the family rosary, our kitchen cupboards seem fairly bare when it comes to food for prayer. And yet, if we look again, there are probably some good quality basic ingredients in there. Language is the bread and butter of most prayer, and many prayer-phrases, blessings, good-wishes, etc., are sprinkled in among our everyday speech, like currants in an oven-soda (for example, God bless! God be good to..., The Lord Save us! God go with you, etc., not to mention the countless Irish language versions, e.g. Dia duit, Dia's Muire duit and so on). By being so close-at-hand, these common expressions bring God into close proximity with what Kavanagh memorably called 'the bits and pieces of everyday'. They are invaluable for bringing God into conversations within kitchens and back-rooms as opposed to the more formal, out-of-home setting of the church building.

HAS YOUR FAMILY EVER GOT TOGETHER TO PRAY THE ROSARY?

NOT FOR DECADES.

If you are fortunate enough to have a child in your home who is following the *Alive-O* programme at school, then you have another very valuable prayer asset. Children following this programme have a wealth of experience of prayer – of many different kinds – and are free of many adult 'hang-ups' about it. They can and should be consulted when help is needed. They are experts. If you don't believe me – ask them a question such as 'Can you show me how to pray?' and see for yourself!

The following three things will be useful:

A Bible
Encourage your family to 'take the Bible into their own hands' in the authoritative sense of that phrase; feel it, look at it, open it, leaf through it, let it become familiar, i.e., 'pertaining to the family'. In some of these prayer-recipes, a biblical story or quotation will be offered, in others you may find greater freedom in choosing your own – or none at all!

Holy Water
Even if it hasn't been blessed, water is a wonderful, blessed thing, one of the four basic elements (the other three being fire, wind and earth). Water supports and nourishes life in so many vital

ways. Its importance for life is reflected in its importance as a Christian symbol especially in the first sacrament we receive – Baptism. Traditionally, Holy Water was much used in the homes of the past. These recipes try to support and develop its continued use as a Christian symbol in our homes.

A Candle
Architects often speak of two kinds of light – living light and dead light. Candles, although they do not give a strong light, do give a living light. Indeed, their popularity of late may in some way be due to an adverse reaction in people to the harshness of so much unnatural light in today's technical world. There is something about a candle which 'catches the eye' of humans and attracts us almost as spontaneously as it attracts moths. Candle-light does not disperse the darkness, but 'warms' it. One need only remember the different kind of living which happens in homes on those rare occasions when the electricity goes off and candles are dotted here and there around the house, and people are literally brought closer together, if only for a short time. Light is another very important Christian symbol, which again, is first introduced in Baptism. Each time a candle is lit in these prayer-recipes, it harks back to Baptism and to Christ as the 'light of the world'.

Spontaneous or Routine?
When many adults say, 'Young people don't pray; they don't go to mass', etc. they are often speaking inaccurately. Many young people do pray and they do go to mass, but not as a matter of routine. Their attention to prayer, of whatever kind, is spontaneous. Like much that is genuine and sincere in life, there is a case to be made for prayer being less routine and more

spontaneous. It is not, and indeed should not, always be the result of a rational decision, but should hopefully be experienced as a kind of reflex action arising in us as a response to a situation or occasion. Therefore, one should not be overly concerned that prayer be said habitually in a family. Rather than aiming for a regular habit, one should try to stay awake and alert, making the most of occasions when it seems like 'the natural thing to do'. A fitting occasion is a vital ingredient, a kind of raising agent in the making of prayer. Then, in retrospect, a family might begin to see a loose pattern forming in the way it prays.

All In Together?
The most common notion of family prayer is one where all members of the family are gathered together in one place at one time. Although, theoretically, this should be easier to achieve today, when families are smaller, in reality it can be very difficult. Younger children may have early bed-times; older children and teenagers tend to be more fully involved in activities outside the home. Homework, meals, favourite TV programmes, phone calls, etc., can mean that time in the evening can be fully booked.

It is difficult and stressful enough for a family to keep various individual timetables moving within one home, as effectively and smoothly as possible, without having the added stress of a mandatory, plenary prayer session each evening. Any effort to impose one is likely to result in hostility to family prayer, something which guarantees diminishing returns for one's efforts. There is the added difficulty of designing a 'prayer' which caters for the different age groups, concentration spans, tastes, and needs, within a family. There are no rules for how often a family should pray together, each family must find out what suits it best, in this regard. The important thing to remember is that it is empowering for a family to know that it can and does come together to pray when the occasion or need or desire arises; it is disempowering for a family to be cramped in a habit whose only real effect is the creation of frustration.

Since a family does not always operate as a whole family, it is important that the activity of praying reflects the various 'bits and pieces' of family. Praying with toddlers at bed-time is legitimate family prayer, i.e., it maintains the 'flow of prayer' on behalf of the total family. Bed-time is probably a good time for praying, because once settled in bed, time is available to focus attention, uninhibited by distractions. Not all children go to bed at the same time, so praying with younger children is an opportunity to focus prayerfully on what is happening in their lives and to give them individual attention. Teenagers and older children will eventually out-grow some of the 'prayer-ways' of younger children, but this is not to say they will out-grow prayer; there may be specific times in their lives, for example, exam times or job-searching, when they are glad to pray and will appreciate the presence, and prayer, of other family members.

Keep It Short
How long or how short prayer should be depends on several factors – the ages of those involved, their experience, their level of 'prayer-fitness', the nature of the occasion, energy levels at the time, etc. In respect of the natural, God-given vivaciousness of children and young people, prayer should not drag. As one's experience of praying grows, so too will one's capacity to recognise when it has reached its natural end. As a rule, prayer is better to be short rather than long.

And finally, to the actual recipes themselves. They are designed to cover a variety of occasions in an average home where to turn to prayer might feel like 'the natural thing to do'. In choosing them, I have avoided occasions such as Easter, Christmas, Baptism, First Communion, Confirmation, anniversaries, etc., which are, in a sense, well taken care of. Someone – usually, but not always, an adult – leads the prayer.

In all of the following prayer recipes, for the sake of expediency I have inserted a name where necessary. You, the reader, will obviously substitute the relevant name instead.

WHEN'S THE LAST
TIME WE KNELT
DOWN TOGETHER
AS A FAMILY?

THAT
TIME
MUM
DROPPED
HER
CONTACT
LENSES
IN THE
GARDEN!

Happy Birthday!

A Thought for 'the Back-of-the-Mind'

> Rejoice in your youth, you who are young
> Let your heart give you joy… (Ecc. 11:9)

or

> For it was you who created my being
> Knit me together in my mother's womb.
> I thank you for the wonder of my being
> For the wonders of all your creation. (Ps 139:13-14)

Ingredients:

> A candle
> The story of the child's birth

There is no story young children like to hear more than the story of their being born. Indeed it is probably one of the best-known and most often-told stories in the life of Jesus. It is a very special story for parents too. It deserves to be told and retold many times. The following prayer is very simply built around the telling of that story. Just as no one person (not even oneself) has the whole story of who one is – there are many aspects to each individual – the story needs to be told in all its versions, i.e., everyone needs to contribute their 'bit' of it.

Time:	Just before the child's bed-time, when normality has returned, and the party guests are long gone home.
Place:	The kitchen.

Invite everyone in the family to gather around the kitchen table. Light the candle.

All:	In the name of the father…, etc.
Leader:	Today is… (name the day and date, e.g. Tuesday 2nd of March)
All Sing:	'Happy Birthday to you…', etc.
Leader:	On this day (five) years ago a new little light, like the light of this candle, came into our lives. It shone and it is still shining. That was a very special day and it has a very special story. Let us tell the story of the day (Peter) was born.

At this point, those present – parent(s), older brothers or sisters, and any grandparents or relatives who may happen to be present – tell, in their own words, their memory of all that happened the day this child was born. They might emphasise how they felt and their reactions on seeing and holding the child for the first time or the kinds of things people said, for example, 'isn't he beautiful; he's the image of...' and recall some of those who came to see him, etc. (It is such a pity that the best things are often said about us when we cannot hear or understand – like when we are newborn babies!)

When everyone present has finished...

Leader:	Let us each think of
	one thing we love about (Peter)
	And thank God for (him).

Those participating can say this aloud, for example, 'Thank God for Peter's laugh!', 'Thank God for Peter's red hair!', etc., or they may simply think about it in silence. While this is happening, if he so wishes, the child whose birthday it is can go around and give each member of the family a hug and say, 'Thank-you'.

When everyone is finished the leader invites everyone to repeat, line by line, the following blessing:

Leader:	God bless (Peter)
	Bless the memory of (his) birth-day
	Guide (him) and keep (him) safe
	Now and always.
Response:	Amen.
Leader:	We ask God to bless all those
	Who are born today
	And those who celebrate their birthday.

May they be blessed with a loving family
To gather round them in celebration.

Response: Amen.

Child whose birthday it is blows out the candle. The others clap.

All: In the name of the father..., etc.

THANK GOD FOR MARY'S LAUGH!

THANK GOD FOR MARY'S HAIR!

THANK GOD WE'VE GOT A BABYSITTER FOR TOMORROW NIGHT SO WE CAN RECOVER FROM MARY'S PARTY!

Exam Time

(This recipe has a Junior Cert/GCSE or Leaving Cert/A-Level student in mind).

A Thought for 'the Back-of-the-Mind'

Do not be afraid – I am with you! (Is 43)

Ingredients: A candle, preferably the student's baptismal candle. The student's exam number and timetable. A Bible.

Time: The evening before the written exams begin.

Place: With her permission, the room in which the student studies. Alternatively, the kitchen or living room.

Invite everyone to gather and find a place to sit in the 'study-space' (the bed or floor of the student's bedroom, if possible). Invite the student to place her exam number and time-table beside the candle.

All: In the name of the father, etc.

Parent: On the day (Elizabeth) was baptised
into the family of God,
we lit (her) baptismal candle.
As we watched it light,
we heard these words,
'This light is entrusted to you to be kept burning brightly.
This child of yours has been enlightened by Christ.'

Family member lights the candle.

This evening, as (Elizabeth) prepares to begin (her) exams
this family re-lights the candle.

Those gathered repeat the following lines after the leader:

(Elizabeth),
in a special way, in the days ahead
we, your family, promise that
we will keep this light, this light of Christ,
burning brightly.
It will be a sign that we, your family,
are with you always.
We also remember all those students
Who will begin exams tomorrow.

Another family member (perhaps a younger child) reads the student's exam number aloud, e.g. 'nine six eight four two nought and says:

This is (Elizabeth)'s exam number.
It is an important number.
This is how (Elizabeth) will be known
to (her) examiners.

Leader: God honours each one of us and calls us by our
name.
In Baptism, you were called by name.
Important though this exam number is,
to your family you will always be
much more than a number.

If they are familiar with it, the family members may sing the well-known psalm, 'Do not be afraid' (No. 122, Hymns Old and New, Kevin Mayhew Publishers) or a reader may read the same piece from Isaiah 43:1-5, or the following version of that reading:

Reader: ...the Lord says...
'Do not be afraid...
I have called you by your name – you are
Mine.
When you pass through deep waters,
I will be with you;
Your troubles will not overwhelm you.
When you pass through fire you will
Not be burnt;
The hard trials that come will not hurt
You.
For I am the Lord your God...

	You are precious to me
	And because I love you and give you
	Honour
	Do not be afraid – I am with you!'
	This is the word of the Lord.
Response:	Thanks be to God.
Leader:	(Elizabeth),
	we your family promise always,
	and especially in the days ahead,
	to remember your name,
	to be with you
	and to keep this light burning brightly for you.
All:	Amen.
Leader:	We remember too that all students have a name
	by which they are called.
	They are all loved
	and cared for by God,
	especially at this time.
Response:	Amen.

At this point, the student may ask the family members to write their names underneath a particular subject in her exam timetable, and to be responsible for lighting the 'exam candle' for this subject. This is done, not in the hope that it will 'get results', but as a sign that the examinee is in their thoughts. The student should put a copy of the exam timetable in a prominent place in the home. When this is finished:

All (to the student): The Lord be with you.
Student: And also with you.
Leader: Let us go in peace.
All: Amen.
    In the name of the Father..., etc.

Awaiting the Results

A Thought for 'the Back-of-the-Mind'

...live as the spirit tells you to... (Rom 8:9)

or

Be sealed with the gift of the Holy Spirit (from the Confirmation ceremony)

Ingredients: A candle
A Bible
A photograph from the student's Confirmation day
A little water
If possible, a special guest, for example, the student's Confirmation sponsor. (He or she might take the role of Leader or Reader).

Time: The evening before the results come out.

Place: Perhaps the living-room, insofar as the rest of the student's life is 'room-for-living', the door to which may open significantly further, tomorrow.

All: In the name of the Father, etc.

As one member of the family lights the candle...

Leader: This evening a candle is being lit,
as it was at the baptism of each member of this family,
and it was again, in Confirmation.
This is an important evening in (Elizabeth)'s life.
(Her) waiting is almost over
We want (her) to know that we are with (her)
as (she) waits through these last hours
'in joyful hope...'

If the family is comfortable with singing, one or all of them could sing 'Be Still and Know'
or
they could take 30-60 seconds to sit quietly and focus on the candle's light and 'experience' the candle. When this is finished, one family member places the Confirmation photograph beside the candle.

Reader (perhaps the student):
When the day of Pentecost came, all the believers were gathered together in one place. Suddenly there was a noise from the sky which sounded like a strong wind blowing, and it filled the whole house where they were sitting. Then they saw

what looked like giant tongues of fire which
spread out and touched each person there. They
were all filled with the Holy Spirit and began to
talk in other languages, as the spirit enabled them
to speak...

Then Peter stood up... and in a loud voice began
to speak...

...'I saw the Lord before me at all times;
he is near me and I will not be troubled.
And so I am filled with gladness,
And my words are full of joy...
You have shown me the paths that
lead to life,
and your presence will fill me with joy'.
(Acts 2:1-5; 14:25-26; 28)
This is the word of the Lord.

Response: Thanks be to God.

Leader: On the day (Elizabeth) was confirmed, we heard
the words:
'All powerful God...
Send your Holy Spirit upon your sons and
daughters
To be their helper and guide.'
(Elizabeth),
important though tomorrow's (seven*) exam
results are
God's Holy Spirit has already 'gifted' you in
(seven) special ways.
On the eve of your exam results,
we your family recall those gifts
and ask the Holy Spirit to nourish that giftedness
at this time in your life.

If they are comfortable doing so, the family members [except the student] could hold out their hands in the way the bishop did at Confirmation, while the following is said:

Leader: (Elizabeth) has been baptised by water and the spirit, and received the Spirit's seven gifts in Confirmation.
            We ask God, to send his Spirit on this water and make it holy so that it may further nourish the gifts of the Spirit in (Elizabeth) and in all students at this time in their lives.
            May God, through the workings of the Holy Spirit, nourish your spirit of wisdom and understanding.

One person makes the sign of the cross on the student's forehead with the Holy Water while the others say...

Response: Help (her) and guide (her)
            that (she) may know what to do
            and have the courage to do it.

Leader: Nourish (her) spirit of knowledge and reverence.

Response: *(signing the cross)*
            Help (her) and guide (her)
            that (she) may come to know and honour
            your presence in her life,
            in the lives of others
            and in the world.

Leader: Nourish (her) spirit of wonder and awe in your presence.

Response: *(signing the cross)*
            Help her and guide her so that

	she may honour the beauty and goodness of all Creation.
Leader:	May the presence of the Gifts of the Spirit in your life and in all lives, bear the fruits of the Spirit May you be blessed with…
Response (All):	Love, Joy, Peace, Patience Kindness, Goodness, Trustfulness, Gentleness, Self-Control.
Leader:	We ask this for Elizabeth and all students who await results at this time and we say
Response:	Our Father…, etc.
Leader:	Peace be with you.
Response:	Peace be with all those who await results of any kind. Amen.
All:	In the name of the Father…, etc.

This should be adapted in a situation of Junior Cert, GCSEs or A-Levels.

PATRICK! COME
DOWN FOR OUR MILLENNIUM
PRAYER SESSION!

MIGHT AS
WELL- MY
COMPUTER'S
STOPPED
WORKING
ANYWAY.

Millennium Moment*

A Thought for 'the Back-of-the-Mind'

...as it was in the beginning,
is now,
and ever shall be
world without end...

or

...our lives ripple through eternity.
Enjoy! (from 'Time is...' by Alan Beam)

or

The most pleasant thing about it [catholicism] is
something like the idea of the communion of
saints, where you can actually talk to your dead. I
like it psychologically, poetically, and if there's a
religious strain in me I would like it in that sense:
I would like to talk to my father, and I would sit
there and talk to the people I've lost, including
the living I have lost. That's what it means to me.
(Brendan Kennelly, *Dark Fathers into Light*, p. 184).

Ingredients:	A sparkler (you might keep one or two of these from Halloween)
	Silence
Time:	Preferably about five minutes before midnight on the eve of the new millennium, though it could be done earlier.
Place:	The kitchen
Leader:	Invite the family to sit in a circle.

Take a moment to give everyone time to make themselves comfortable. Switch out all lights. In a soft, quiet voice ask everyone to be silent and still. Light the sparkler★
Allow about 30 seconds of complete silence as people watch the sparks burst into life, shoot into the air and fall. Then in a soft voice, the leader may explain the following in his or her own words:

Leader:	The sparks which shoot from the sparkler are like the lives of all those who have gone before us – very brief, but brilliantly bright 'lights-in-the-dark'. As we watch them we remember deceased relatives and friends and indeed, dead generations we never knew. We put ourselves in touch with them.

Invite those who wish, to whisper the name of a deceased person (or an absent family member) they would like to remember as the sparkler burns to the end. When the sparks have been exhausted, the light is switched on.

Leader:	(*again explains in his or her own words that*):
	As we switch on the lights, we are in the here-and-now. This is the present, the new millennium; this is where we are; we are the light-for-now; we are the light for the moment, for the new-millennium-moment.
Reader:	'I know that everything God does will live forever. You can't add anything to it or take anything away from it... Whatever happens or can happen has already happened before.'
	(Ecc 3:14-15)
or	
	'Before the world was created, the Word already existed; he was with God, and he was the same as God. From the very beginning the Word was with God. Through him God made all things; not one thing in all creation was made without him. The Word was the source of life, and this life brought light to humankind. The light shines in the darkness, and the darkness has never put it out.' (Jn 1:1-6)
	This is the word of the Lord.
Response:	Thanks be to God.

If you have children following the Alive-O programme at school, some of them may know and sing repeatedly, 'Time and time and time again, Praise God, praise God'.

Leader:	Lord God,
	as we pray here, together
	on the eve of the new millennium,

as we remember deceased generations,
we ask you to bring
them and us
and those who will come after us
into the light of your presence
where we may live
for ever and ever.

Response: Glory be to the Father
And to the Son
And to the Holy Spirit
As it was in the beginning
Is now
And ever shall be
World without end
Amen.
In the name of the Father..., etc.

This prayer could easily be adapted to suit the feasts of All Souls and All Saints or the anniversary of a deceased relative.

IS THIS THE HOUSE WHERE YOU'RE HOLDING THE PRAYER SESSION FOR THE NEW BABY?

GUEST INVITE

Welcome Home For A New Baby

A Thought for 'the Back-of-the-Mind'

...trailing clouds of glory do we come
From God, who is our home:
Heaven lies about us in our infancy! (from
'Imitations of Immortality' from *Recollections of
Early Childhood* by William Wordsworth)

or

But there is a way of life
that is its own witness:
put the kettle on, shut the blind.
Home is a sleeping child,
An open mind
and our effects,
shrugged and settled
in the sort of light
jugs and kettles
grow important by.
(from 'Domestic Interior' by Eavan Boland)

Ingredients:	A candle
	A special blanket
	Holy water in a small jug or dish
	Perhaps some special guests – e.g. the baby's grandparents

| Time: | The baby's first evening 'home'. |

| Place: | The warmest room in the house. |

Invite the family to sit in a circle, with the baby in a cot in the centre.

All:	In the name of the Father…, etc.
Leader:	This is a happy day.
	We are gathered together to welcome
	our new baby into our family.
	We have waited and waited,
	but now our waiting is over.
	This is a happy day.
	Lift up your hearts.
Response:	We have raised them up to the Lord.
Leader:	Let us give thanks to the Lord our God.
Response:	It is right to give God thanks and praise.

If there are school-children in the family, they might like, at this point, to sing 'Céad Míle Fáilte Romhat A Íosa', (substituting the word 'leanbh' for 'Íosa' on this occasion).
or
Those present might sing an 'Alleluia'.

| Leader: | Blessed are you Lord God of all Creation. |

Through your goodness
We have new life
the new life of this baby.
Response: Blessed be God forever.

I. BLESSING THE BABY

Invite those gathered to stand. Each time the following litany response is spoken, someone steps forward and, dipping a finger in the Holy Water, blesses the baby as is appropriate.

Leader: May God bless this baby –
               Bless (his) eyes
               that they may always see the goodness
               in (himself)
               in others
               in the world,
               and begin to know God.
Response: God bless (him). *(Someone makes the sign of the cross on the baby's eyelids, or thereabouts!)*
Leader: Bless (his) ears
               that they may hear stories
               told in the voices of those around (him)
               and begin to know God.
Response: God bless (him). *(Someone blesses the baby's ears.)*
Leader: Bless (his) nose
               that it may smell
               the scent and perfumes
               of Nature and Creation
               and begin to know God.
Response: God bless (him). *(Someone blesses the baby's nose.)*

Leader:	Bless (his) mouth
	that (he) may taste
	the food of life
	and begin to know God.
Response:	God bless (him). *(Someone blesses the baby's mouth.)*
Leader:	Bless (his) hands and feet
	that they may keep (him)
	in touch
	with the earth
	and with others
	and begin to know God.
Response:	God bless (him). *(Someone blesses the baby's hands and feet.)*

WELL YOU DID INSIST ON BEING THE ONE TO BLESS THE BABY'S MOUTH...

FIRST AID

Leader: We welcome this baby
into this family.
We look forward to (his) life with us.
We promise to love and care for (him) always.
We also look back
and remember former generations of this family
who have died.
We ask them to be here with us today
and bless this baby
as they too welcome (him) into this family.

At this point the leader could invite anyone who is old enough to remember a grand-uncle or aunt or other relative of the family and think of what they were blessed with, then pass that blessing on to the baby, for example, 'May (he) be blessed with Uncle Michael's singing voice', 'May (he) be blessed with Aunt Anna's way with flowers and plants', 'May (he) be blessed with Granny Rose's way with stories', etc. Those who are not old enough to do this may pass on a blessing of someone in the wider family who they know.

AND MAY THE WHOLE FAMILY REMEMBER THE WARMTH OF ITS LOVE BY NOT RUNNING UP HUGE CENTRAL HEATING BILLS.

III. WRAPPING THE BABY IN THE WARMTH OF FAMILY LOVE

One member of the family – possibly a grandparent – holds the baby and wraps the blanket around him.

Leader:	We praise and thank God
	for the gift of this new life in our family.
	We remember God's love for us
	and we wrap this blanket around our baby
	as a sign of the warmth and love
	with which we will cherish (him)
	all the days of our lives.
Response:	Amen.
Leader:	May all newborn children
	who make their home debut today,
	find themselves blanketed
	in the warmth of a loving family.
Response:	Amen.

If they are comfortable singing, the family might sing any hymn which speaks of the love of God, e.g. 'Love is his Word' or, if there are Alive-O children in the family they could sing, 'Thank you God we Love You.'

All:	In the name of the Father…, etc.

Toddling Prayers!

Prayer is essentially an inhaling and exhaling of breath by an aspirator, as opposed to a respirator – a machine which substitutes for the natural breathing process. In the Bible, the words 'breath' and 'spirit' are quite interchangeable. Although 'to aspire' is generally understood in an ambitious sense, its older meaning is to breathe, to rise up high, as does breath or smoke (or bubbles). I suggest that one directly spiritual way in which the child plays is blowing bubbles. For an adult, the act of praying is not unlike the action of the child blowing bubbles: the adult dips into some worry or joy or other 'moving' experience and breathes certain words of prayer onto that experience, causing it to be released and rise high, a perfect, ephemeral sphere of light and breath and spirit. In the following recipe, the overlapping of blessing and blowing/breathing is a combination of images and words in a playful, prayerful way in the life of the toddler. The litany form, which the blessing takes, is one of the oldest known prayer-forms, much loved by our early Irish ancestors. In its content too, the litany resonates with Celtic-Christian spirituality, which saw God's blessing in the most simple and natural things in everyday life.

A Thought for 'the Back-of-the-Mind'

> ...he breathed life-giving breath... (Gen 2:7)
> Then he breathed on them and said, 'Receive the Holy Spirit... (Jn 20:22)

or

Blowing Bubbles

> Hold a magic bubble wand
> Close up to the mouth
> To ease a bubble out.

If the bubble quivers
And shivers in its skin
And wants to grow; but can't let go
And clings on its rim
Then breathe a tiny warm breath
Friendly, full and fat
And see the little bubble grow
And grow, and burst! That's that!

Ingredients: A little tub of bubbles

Place/Time: Anywhere, anytime, but perhaps in the morning
in the garden or in the evening in the child's
bedroom.

The age at which children can actually blow bubbles varies, but whether they can or not, it is something every child enjoys being involved in. If the child cannot blow bubbles, it is important nevertheless that he or she is encouraged to try; the adult may help out. The wording offered is merely a suggestion, the child should bless whoever and whatever he or she thinks of; the order in which they are blessed is not important.

Leader & Child: Blow…
God bless Granny
Blow…
God bless Grandad
Blow…
God bless (family members)
Blow…
God bless (relations)
Blow…

God bless the cat/dog/the birds in their nests/ the hills/the fields/the streets/the beds that we sleep in/the bread that we eat/the music that we hear/the worms in the garden/the bubbles we blow, etc.
Amen.

Gone to Hospital

The particular prayer recipe offered here does not attempt to deal with situations where the Sacrament of the Sick is obviously what is appropriate. Instead, it envisages a situation where, for example, a family member requires hospitalisation for a short time, but is not in danger. However, a family often feels a child's or a parent's absence or separation from the family, in a particularly poignant way when it is due to illness. This recipe seeks to offer prayerful recognition of that feeling of 'missing presence'.

A Thought for 'the Back-of-the-Mind'

> How many times have I wanted to put my arms around all your people, just as a hen gathers her chicks under her wings... (Matt 23:37)

or

> Remain in me, as I in you.
> As a branch cannot bear fruit all by itself
> Unless you remain in me. (Jn 15:4-5)

Ingredients: A candle
                 A Bible
                 An empty chair

Time: On the first night of the person's being in hospital.

Place: The kitchen, or whatever room is considered to be the heart or hub of the home.

Invite all those present to sit in a circle. Include an empty chair to represent the person who is missing.

All: In the name of the Father…, etc.

One member of the family lights the candle – if possible the Baptismal candle of the person concerned.

Leader: As we light this candle
                      we remember the candle that was lit at (Kevin)'s
                      baptism
                      when (he) became a member of God's family.
                      We remember (his) birthday candles
                      which this family lit to celebrate (his) birthdays.
                      This evening, as we sit here,
                      we are aware of the empty chair.
                      We feel (Kevin)'s absence from our family.
                      As we light this candle
                      we bring (Kevin) to mind
                      and we listen to the comforting words of Jesus:
Reader   'For only a penny you can buy two sparrows, yet
                      not one sparrow falls to the ground without your
                      father's consent. As for you, even the hairs of
                      your head have all been counted. So do not be
                      afraid; you are worth much more than sparrows!'
Or in the case of an absent child:
                      'Some people brought children to Jesus for him to
                      place his hands on them, but disciples scolded the
                      people. When Jesus noticed this he was angry
                      and said to the disciples, "Let the children come
                      to me, and do not stop them…" Then he took the

children in his arms, placed his hands on each one of them and blessed them.' (Mk 10:13-17)
This is the word of the Lord.

Response: Thanks be to God.

The leader, in his or her own words, invites the family to sit quietly and still, close their eyes, and settle their minds. If there are Alive-O children in the house who know 'Quiet and Still', they could be invited to sing it now. Speaking softly, the leader continues, again in his or her own words or in the following words:

Leader: Picture the hospital ward. Feel how quiet it is. Listen to the sound of people's breathing as they sleep. Hear the various sounds of a hospital – feet coming and going down corridors, trolleys rattling, phones ringing in the distance, etc. Feel that kind of hospital-warmth; smell that hospital-smell. Move into the ward/room. Look for (Kevin)'s bed. Go over to it; see all of us gathered around it. Reach out and take (Kevin)'s hand. How is (he)?... What would you like to say to (him)?... What does (he) say to you?... Imagine Jesus is there too... What does Jesus say/do?... Stay there for a moment or two with (Kevin).

The leader allows for a short pause, mindful of the short concentration span of any young child who may be taking part. The leader now invites the family to return 'home'; slowly opening their eyes and (particularly for the sake of young children), stretching themselves before continuing.

Leader:	Although (Kevin) is not sitting here with us,
	we are with (him) in other ways
	and (he) is with us.
	God is with us too.
	The Holy Spirit, given to us in Baptism and Confirmation
	is also with us.
	The Risen Jesus is present with us too,
	He is present with us in a special way in the mass.
	In a special way, (Kevin) is with us as we pray
	And repeat the words of the mass:

Family repeats after the leader:

Father,
Hear the prayers of the family
Gathered here before you.
In mercy and love unite all your children,
Wherever they may be.

Other family members say the following:

Prayer:	Remember (Kevin) and all those who are in hospital tonight.
Response:	God be with them and bless them.
Prayer:	Remember their families who miss them.
Response:	God be with them and bless them.
Prayer:	Remember all those who work in hospitals,
	to bring people well-being.
Response:	God be with them and bless them.
Prayer:	Remember all those who work in homes and communities
	to bring people well-being.
Response:	God be with them and bless them.

Prayer:	Remember those throughout the world, who have not got the help and healing they are in need of.
Response:	God be with them and bless them.
Leader:	We are (Kevin)'s family. Let us keep this light Burning brightly in our thoughts, for (him) and for all those in hospital during the days / weeks ahead until (he) is back with us again.
All:	Amen. In the name of the Father…, etc.

LET'S ALL PRAY THAT
DADDY WILL BE OUT OF
HOSPITAL SOON … AND
THAT NEXT TIME HE FINDS
YOU ALL BEHAVING
YOURSELVES AND PRAYING
THE SHOCK WON'T BE
AS TRAUMATIC …

Home Again, Home Again!

As its name suggests, the following recipe seeks to celebrate a family member's return home from hospital. It is a very simple recipe.

It should be emphasised that, although it overlaps with healing, this recipe is aimed at celebrating the restoration of family togetherness. It seeks not to 'overwhelm' the individual who has been absent by keeping the recipe as close to what would be normal in the home as possible. This is prayer at its most 'natural'.

The candle is placed in the middle of the table, marking this as a special meal and a special celebration. The person's hospital tag could be placed alongside the candle. There might also be some special food.

A Thought for the Back-of-the-Mind

> It is the living who praise you,
> As I praise you now...
> Lord you have healed me.
> We will play harps and sing your praise...
> (Is 38:19-20)

or

> Jesus used parables to tell all these things to the crowds;
> he would not say a thing to them without using a parable. (Matt 13:34)

Ingredients: A candle
                   Hospital wrist-tag

Time: First evening home from hospital

Place: Around the kitchen table which has been laid, ready for tea or dinner or supper.

All:	In the name of the Father…, etc.
Leader:	*(as the candle is lit)*
	Bless us O God
	As we sit and eat,
	All of us,
	Together Again!
All:	Amen.

As the meal is being eaten and, having due regard for the fact that the person in question may be feeling tired, he should be invited to tell his story – as much or as little as he feels able to. He might like to mention other people who were in the ward (patients and staff) and snippets of their stories too. (Each individual's story is always overlapping with other people's stories; our own story is always part of a much bigger one).

When the story has been told, the others might tell something of what has been happening at home. (Probably not a lot, but it is important, for the one who was absent, that it be told).

When the tea/dinner/supper is over:

Leader:	Thanks be to God
	For the food we have eaten;
	For the company we have shared;
	For the stories we have heard.
	Thanks be to God
	We are all together again.
Response:	Amen.
	In the name of the Father…, etc.

St Brigid

There are different ways in which the following recipe could be 'made'.
It could be carried out by a little 'procession' – perhaps a St Brigid's
cross, followed by a lighted candle, followed by some Holy Water –
passing through the house, blessing its various parts. However, I suspect
that it might fit more realistically into the middle of a morning's house-
work! The suggestion, therefore, is that it be enacted as one 'goes one's
rounds', cleaning and tidying, perhaps with the help of any preschool
children in the home. There is a quiet kind of 'in-touchness' that comes
with the handling of the domestic intimacies of a house and home. St
Brigid has special blessings to offer via these intimacies and details.

A Thought for the Back-of-the-Mind

> For Brigid: Mary of Ireland
> You usher in the spring
> You welcome all who visit
> You shelter the poor in your cloak
> You inspire writers and singers
> You strengthen workers in metal-work
> You guide the hands of healers
> You soften the hate that divides
> You cherish what comes to birth
> You mirror Jesus in your life
> (by Tom Hamill, adapted).

Ingredients: If possible, a St Brigid's Cross
             Holy Water

Time: The morning of St Brigid's Day.

Place: Throughout the house.

(sprinkle Holy Water with each blessing)
May St Brigid bless this window
so that,
in appreciation of the fresh air
and light
that it brings to this family,
they may give God thanks and praise.
Response: Blessed be St Brigid.

II BLESSING FOR A BED

May St Brigid bless this bed
So that,
in finding rest and peace,
those who sleep in it
may give thanks to God.
Response: Blessed be St Brigid.

I THINK ST BRIGID WOULD LIKE ME TO POINT OUT THAT IN ORDER TO BLESS YOUR BED YOU HAVE TO GET OUT OF IT FIRST!

May St Brigid bless this table
so that
those who gather around it to eat
may taste goodness in every bite
and give God thanks and praise.

Response: Blessed be St Brigid.

May St Brigid bless these taps
so that
every drop of water
that flows from them
may refresh
in body and soul
those in this house
so that they give God thanks and praise.

Response: Blessed be St Brigid.

THIS 'BLESSING OF TAPS' IS MIRACULOUS – FIRST TIME THE BACK OF OUR SON'S EARS HAVE BEEN NEAR WATER FOR DAYS!

IV BLESSING FOR A HEARTH

May St Brigid bless this hearth
so that
those who gather around
every fire that is kindled in it
may feel warmth and love
and give God thanks and praise.

Response: Blessed be St Brigid.

VI BLESSING FOR WALLS

May St Brigid bless these walls
so that
those who live within them
may find safety, security and shelter
and give God thanks and praise.

Response: Blessed be St Brigid

Find a place to hang the St Brigid's Cross. Sprinkle it with Holy Water as the final prayer is said.

VII BLESSING FOR THE FAMILY

May St Brigid
bless us all
so that our lives
give God thanks and praise.

Response: Blessed be St Brigid
Amen.

An Afterthought

For all who take on the making of these recipes.

...And One For...
Mother.
She has measured out her life
in teaspoons.
Wee spoon after teaspoon
of babies' solid food –
spuds and milk,
salt and butter,
mashed on a saucer
fed in the oral
tradition of the mother
tongue. Mouth-to-mouth
the kiss of life
to the Gospel of Christ.
'If you love me, feed my lambs,
feed my sheep'. Amen.
...and...
one for – its mother....